William's Turn

Written and Illustrated by
Anna Grossnickle Hines

Children's Press®
A Division of Scholastic Inc.
New York • Toronto • London • Auckland • Sydney
Mexico City • New Delhi • Hong Kong
Danbury, Connecticut

To Martha
—A. G. H.

Reading Consultants
Linda Cornwell
Coordinator of School Quality and Professional Improvement
(Indiana State Teachers Association)

Katharine A. Kane
Education Consultant
(Retired, San Diego County Office of Education
and San Diego State University)

Visit Children's Press® on the Internet at:
http://publishing.grolier.com

Library of Congress Cataloging-in-Publication Data

Hines, Anna Grossnickle.
    William's turn / written and illustrated by Anna Grossnickle Hines.
        p. cm. — (Rookie reader)
    Summary: William does not join the other children in playing games on the
playground because he is waiting for his turn to ring the bell at the end of
recess.
    ISBN 0-516-22177-9 (lib. bdg.)   0-516-25969-5 (pbk.)
    [1. Playgrounds—Fiction.] I. Title. II. Series.
PZ7.H572 Wo 2001
[E]—dc21   00-047376

© 2001 by Anna Grossnickle Hines
Printed in the United States of America.
1 2 3 4 5 6 7 8 9 10 R 10 09 08 07 06 05 04 03 02 01

Bob and Brandon bounced a ball.

Rose and Ruby ran a race.

Jamal and Jenny jumped ten times.

William waited for his turn.
Now?

Not yet.

Rose and Ruby bounced a ball.

Jamal and Jenny ran a race.

Bob and Brandon
jumped twenty times.

William waited for his turn.
Now?

Not yet.

Jamal and Jenny bounced a ball.

Bob and Brandon ran a race.

Rose and Ruby jumped thirty times.

William waited for his turn.

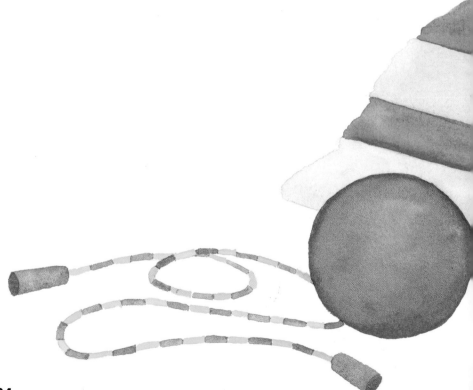

Now?

Now.

William rang the bell.

And everyone came running!

Word List (32 words)

a	everyone	race	thirty
and	for	ran	times
ball	his	rang	turn
bell	Jamal	Rose	twenty
Bob	Jenny	Ruby	waited
bounced	jumped	running	William
Brandon	not	ten	William's
came	now	the	yet

About the Author and Illustrator

Anna Grossnickle Hines's career with children began in the classroom, teaching preschool and third grade. Then she turned her creative talents to writing and illustrating children's books. Many of the more than fifty books she has written and/or illustrated have received awards and honors. You can visit her website at www.aghines.com.